the Warrior in the Mirror

A Bible Study Journal for Busy Women

Hebrews 4:14-16
Therefore, since we have a great high priest who has passed through the heavens, Jesus the Son of God, let us hold fast our confession. For we do not have a high priest who cannot sympathize with our weaknesses, but One who has been tempted in all things as we are, yet without sin. Therefore let us draw near with confidence to the throne of grace, so that we may receive mercy and find grace to help in time of need.

Dedicated to all of the incredible ladies, whom God has placed in my life. I can't think of anyone else I'd rather do life with!

Soli deo Gloria

The Warrior in the Mirror - a Bible Study Journal For Busy Women

Jellybean Jar Publications
1212 11th. St. E.
Glencoe, MN
55336

© 2016 by Angela O'Dell
Cover image from Shutterstock.com

ISBN-13: 978-1530615315
ISBN -10: 1530615313

You can find more information about Angela O'Dell on the web:
blog: angelaodellblog.wordpress.com
website: jellybeanjar.org
Facebook: Angela O'Dell's Jellybean Jar Publications Facebook Page
email: angela@jellybeanjar.org

"Put your sweet self under God. Entirely.
No arms and legs kicking out to the sides.
Knees to the floor. Eyes to the sky!
Hands open wide. Death to pride. Here we
run aground on the reason the devil flees. He
doesn't flee from us, Beloved. He runs from
God, Who is standing right there over us
every time we submit. Take off your shoes -
that's holy ground."

Beth Moore - James

James - Mercy Triumphs by Beth Moore
published by LifeWay Press® ©Beth Moore
reprint 2014

James 1 Message

2-4 Consider it a sheer gift, friends, when testing and challenges come at you from all sides. You know that under pressure, your faith-life is forced into the open and shows its true colors. So don't try to get out of anything prematurely. Let it do its work so you become mature and well-developed, not deficient in any way.

22-24 Don't fool yourself by thinking that you are a listener, when you are anything but, letting the Word go in one ear and out the other. Act on what you hear! Those who hear and don't act are like those who glance in the mirror, walk away, and two minutes later have no idea who they are, or what they look like.

Dear Friend,

This is not a buck-up-and-put-on-a-brave-face pep-talk book...

This precious life can be such a mix of triumph and trial. As I write this, I'm thinking about a dear, brave friend, who is facing an excruciating time in her life. For more than two years, she has been standing by her husband as he battles cancer. She has three children to think about, and the future is uncertain to say the least. This sweet friend is hanging onto Jesus with everything she has. Every day brings new challenges; each morning, she gets up to face what is now her reality. She isn't doing it in her own strength - that ran out a long time ago - no, she is living in the shadow of the Almighty's wing. I'm so thankful she knows where her strength comes from.

I believe, as women of God, we have a lot more "guts" than what we tell ourselves and each other most of the time, but it requires determination to take God at His Word when we don't feel like it. It's easier and more natural for us to whine and complain, or blame it on our hormones than it is to dig in and stand strong. The enemy of our souls cashes in on these tendencies more often than we want to admit. He knows that if he can distract us from our Power Source, he has rendered a great army of warriors ineffectual.

BUT...

What if we became the kind of women who takes every thought captive and lives in strength and humility? What if we believed what God says about us? What if we looked into the mirror and truly saw a mighty warrior, armed for battle? What if we disciplined ourselves to meet with God every day (morning preferably) to align ourselves with HIS plans for the day?

God's Word says that we have access to everything we need, to not just get through, but to come out victoriously on the other side. Christ has died so that we can live in victory. Whomever the Son has set free, is free indeed! Freedom is sweet!

About me:

God has delivered me from some horrifically bad places, and He continues to use His Word to heal me. He has taught me to replace the lies of Satan with the truth of what He says about me and to take every thought captive. He has given me a passion to share the source of my strength and joy. If He can heal and use me, believe me, He can heal and use anybody!

This book is a glimpse of my personal morning routine with Jesus. I have included all of the (somewhat quirky but effective) elements of what I do on a daily basis to focus my heart and mind on the One who owns the day that I am about to live. It is from my own thankfulness for the power of Christ that I bring you this book. Please use it in the way it fits your needs. Over the next few pages, I explain the layout of this journal and give some helps for your journey. Please take the time to read through it all. God bless!

About this book

Following is a breakdown of the sections in this journal and how I use them in my quiet times.

Praise song or hymn: this is pretty self explanatory. Usually, I listen to a hymn or praise song in my earbuds while I hug my cup of coffee.

"Face-time" with Jesus: this is my face-to-the-floor time - putting myself in a position of complete humbleness before God. I have found when I take the time to put myself completely on my face before God, my attitudes and thoughts quiet themselves and my mind shifts to the greatness of His presence. Sometimes I stay down a few minutes, sometimes I stay down there longer if I have something that is keeping me from quieting my thoughts. "Humble yourself before God. Resist the devil and he will flee." (If you cannot physically go face-down on the floor, please choose a position that works for you. This is a heart position much more than a physical position.)

PRAY: I like to use this acronym.

Praise- Thank and praise God for His greatness and faithfulness in my life. I praise Him completely for being who He says He is and doing what He says He will do.

Repent: This may be something that I need to do first even before praising. If He brings something to my mind that needs to be taken care of, I do it now!

Ask: Do I need to ask my Heavenly Father for something? Scripture says to pour out our hearts to Him. Ask!

Yes! Stand on the promises of who He says I am. I pray the Scriptures over my family and home. I have included a short list of books that I use for praying the Scriptures.

People or situations I need to trust God about: Trust...not something that comes to us naturally. Most of us have endured enough injustice at the hands of humans to be a little leery of those who have power over us.

If you have trust issues, ask God to show you how trustworthy He truly is. There is no dark side to His nature. We all have people/issues/situations that we have to daily (and sometimes moment-by-moment) lay at His feet in surrender. This has been a big one for me - I have to conscientiously lay it down and leave it there. Live with open hands.

Scripture writing: If you are following a specific scripture writing plan, this is a great place to write out the verses. (These verses can also come from an in-depth Bible study I may be doing, a devotional, or Scripture that I jotted down in church. The idea here is to write out God's Word in our own handwriting. There is something powerful about writing something down.)

Application: This is where I write what is God showing me from my scripture reading. God's Word is alive and active, sharper than a two-edged sword. It is good for all types of training and admonition. (Hebrews 4:12, 2 Timothy 3:16)

Other verses I read: I jot down the references of other scriptures I read and ponder each day. These sometimes become my handwritten scripture on another day.

Armor check list: Before I end my quiet time, I take a moment and put on my Spiritual armor.

Don't start the day without suiting up. (Ephesians 6:10-18) I've included this checklist because I have found it helpful to consciously work through the process of applying each piece of armor's truth to myself. Jesus died to give us this privilege - let's not go without its protection and defensive/offensive power!

Other journaling/doodling/areas: I like to color and doodle. In fact, I have realized that this activity can not only calm my mind and spirit, but it can actually be a form of praise and worship! (I know that I'm not alone in this by how popular journaling Bible and adult coloring books have become lately.) Many times, I will doodle or color when I'm listening to a hymn or a praise song. Please don't feel like you have to be an artist to participate in this activity. Your journal is for you to document your time with Jesus - make it yours!

Some of my favorite resources for Bible study and Prayer books:

Fervent by Priscilla Shirer

Praying God's Word by Beth Moore

60 Promises to Pray Over Your Children by Roy Lessin

Praying for Prodigals by James Bank

The Armor of God Bible Study by Priscilla Shirer

Breaking Free Bible Study by Beth Moore

(Any of the studies by Beth Moore, Priscilla Shirer, Angela Thomas)

Favorite online resource: www.biblehub.com

Ideas...

Here are some suggestions for using this quiet-time/prayer journal:

- Use the journal in conjunction with a daily devotional. My favorites are "Experiencing God Day by Day," by Henry Blackaby, "Then Sings My Soul," (any and all of the volumes) by Robert J. Morgan, and "Streams in the Desert," by L.B. Cowman - updated by James Reimann.

- If you are a mother of a struggling, young-adult child, I invite you to join me as I, too, use this journal in my journey through the book, "Praying for Prodigals," by James Bank, as I battle for my 22 year old son's heart and soul.

- If you are a wife, or planning on getting married soon, I recommend a little book by Gwen Ford Faulkenberry, "60 Promises to Pray For Your Marriage."

- If you are a mom with a house full of littles - or even if it just feels full - you'll love one of my favorite praying-the-Word resources, "60 Promises to Pray Over Your Children," by Roy Lessin.

- If you are a woman who longs to become a prayer warrior, you NEED to read and journal through Priscilla Shirer's book, "Fervent."

- If you want a fresh focus to pray and journal through every month, I invite you to visit the "Monthly Focus" page on my blog: angelaodellblog.wordpress.com. Each month, I post a new prayer focus, Scripture writing focus, and study focus.

- Or you can simply choose a book from the Word of God to study in depth. Pray, write, journal, and learn, as the Holy Spirit brings the Word to life.

Prayers lifted: ▼

answers received: ↘

Your will be done, Lord!

The Truth About Me...

----------→ truth = what God says about everything

Ephesians 1

I am equipped through Christ with every spiritual blessing.

I am chosen in Him before the foundations of the world.

I am regarded as holy and blameless before Him.

I am adopted through the kind intention of His will.

I am redeemed and forgiven, lavished with grace.

I am a recipient of a glorious inheritance in heaven.

I am secured forever by the Holy Spirit of promise.

I am alive with the Messiah - together with Christ Jesus seated at the right hand of the throne.

I am a dearly loved child of God.

Hymn or song _____

_____

_____

◯ face-time with Jesus

This is Your day, Lord, and I am Yours in it!

Pray:
& Praise _____

_____

Repent:
& He will give peace _____

_____

Ask:
pour out your heart _____

_____

Yes:
stand on His promises _____

_____

Doodles & Notes

He makes all things beautiful in His time.

Jesus, I trust you with... _____

_____

_____

_____

_____

Handwritten Scripture

_____
_____
_____
_____
_____
_____
_____
_____
_____

what I learned

_____
_____
_____
_____

☆ armor check

the belt of truth – stand firm on what God says!

the breastplate of righteousness – holiness given/holiness lived.

the shoes of peace – stand firm, spread the news!

the shield of faith – be obedient in faith!

the helmet of salvation – take every thought captive.

the sword of the Spirit – learn to wield the Word of God.

On the third day, He will come like rain.
Hosea 6:3

hymn or song:
_____
_____

◯ face-time with Jesus

P R
A Y & **P R A I S E**
_____
_____

R E
P E
N T receive forgiveness
_____

A
S
K He hears
_____

Y
E
S Thank you, Jesus!
_____

HE MAKES BEAUTY FROM ASHES ──→
JESUS, I TRUST YOU WITH:

Notes & Doodles

_____
_____
_____
_____

Handwritten Scripture

what I learned

armor check

the belt of truth – stand firm on what God says!

the breastplate of righteousness – holiness given/holiness lived.

the shoes of peace – stand firm, spread the news!

the shield of faith – be obedient in faith!

the helmet of salvation – take every thought captive.

the sword of the Spirit – learn to wield the Word of God.

This hope is a strong and trustworthy anchor for our souls. It leads us through the curtain into God's inner sanctuary.
Hebrews 6:19

hymn or song:
_____
_____
_____

▲ ☐ face-time with Jesus

Pray: _____
& Praise
_____

Repent: _____
He gives grace
_____

Ask: _____
& He will answer
_____

Yes: _____
He will never leave you
_____

Our struggle is not against flesh and blood.
Jesus, I trust you with:

Notes & Doodles

_____
_____
_____
_____
_____

Handwritten Scripture

_____

_____

_____

_____

_____

_____

_____

_____

what I learned...

_____

_____

_____

_____

☆ armor check

the belt of truth – stand firm on what God says!

the breastplate of righteousness – holiness given/holiness lived.

the shoes of peace – stand firm, spread the news!

the shield of faith – be obedient in faith!

the helmet of salvation – take every thought captive.

the sword of the Spirit – learn to wield the Word of God.

Grace received...Grace given.

_____
_____
_____

◯ **face-time with Jesus**

Pray: _____
  & **P**raise
_____

Repent: _____
He will come like the rain
_____
_____

Ask: _____
let your request be known
_____
_____

Yes: _____
He's a good Father
_____
_____

Mercy Triumphs
JESUS, I TRUST YOU WITH:

◀ **Notes & Doodles**

_____
_____
_____
_____
_____
_____

Handwritten Scripture

What I Learned Today...

◯ armor check

the belt of truth – stand firm on what God says!
the breastplate of righteousness – holiness given/holiness
lived.
the shoes of peace – stand firm, spread the news!
the shield of faith – be obedient in faith!
the helmet of salvation – take every thought captive.
the sword of the Spirit – learn to wield the Word of God.

BLESSED IS SHE
WHOSE STRENGTH
IS THE LORD!

face time with Jesus

Pray:
& Praise

Repent:
His blood covers it all

Ask:
and you will receive

Yes:
His blessings are amazing

Control is an illusion God has it.
Jesus, I trust you with:

Notes & Doodles

Handwritten Scripture

what I learned

◯ armor check

the belt of truth – stand firm on what God says!

the breastplate of righteousness – holiness given/holiness lived.

the shoes of peace – stand firm, spread the news!

the shield of faith – be obedient in faith!

the helmet of salvation – take every thought captive.

the sword of the Spirit – learn to wield the Word of God.

Hymn or Song _____

_____

➡ face-time with Jesus

Blessed is she whose strength is in the Lord.

Pray: _____

& Praise _____

Repent: _____

strength is in forgiveness _____

Ask: _____

the Shepherd gives us what we need _____

Yes: _____

take Him at His Word _____

NOTES & DOODLES

Jesus, I trust you with...
Your grace is sufficient.

_____

_____

_____

_____

Handwritten Scripture

_____

_____

_____

_____

_____

_____

_____

_____

_____

_____

what I learned ⟶ _____

_____

_____

_____

_____

☐ ARMOR CHECK

the belt of truth – stand firm on what God says!

the breastplate of righteousness – holiness given/holiness lived.

the shoes of peace – stand firm, spread the news!

the shield of faith – be obedient in faith!

the helmet of salvation – take every thought captive.

the sword of the Spirit – learn to wield the Word of God.

Hymn or song _____

_____

_____

face-time with Jesus

Dare to live in the freedom Christ died to give you.

Pray: _____
& Praise
_____

_____

Repent: _____
give it to Jesus
_____

_____

Ask: _____
He is listening
_____

_____

Yes: _____
His plan is good
_____

_____

He loves me, this I know.

Doodles & Notes

JESUS, I TRUST YOU WITH... _____

_____

_____

_____

_____

Handwritten Scripture

_____

_____

_____

_____

_____

_____

_____

_____

_____

_____

_____

what I learned

_____

_____

_____

_____

○ armor check

the belt of truth – stand firm on what God says!

the breastplate of righteousness – holiness given/holiness lived.

the shoes of peace – stand firm, spread the news!

the shield of faith – be obedient in faith!

the helmet of salvation – take every thought captive.

the sword of the Spirit – learn to wield the Word of God.

Hymn or song

_____

face-time with Jesus

Sadness to joy
Tiredness to dancing.
Sin-sick to healed.
All because of Jesus

Pray:
& Praise _____

Repent: _____
Create in me a clean heart!

Ask: _____
all I have needed, Your hand has provided

Yes: _____
Your Word is light to my path

notes & doodles

Jesus, I trust you with...
He is our peace.

_____

_____

_____

_____

_____

Handwritten Scripture

what I learned

☐ **armor check**

the belt of truth – stand firm on what God says!

the breastplate of righteousness – holiness given/holiness lived.

the shoes of peace – stand firm, spread the news!

the shield of faith – be obedient in faith!

the helmet of salvation – take every thought captive.

the sword of the Spirit – learn to wield the Word of God.

Hymn or song _____

_____

_____

This is Your day, Lord, and I am yours in it!

◯ face-time with Jesus

Pray: _____
& Praise
_____

_____

Repent: _____
& He will give peace
_____

_____

Ask: _____
pour out your heart
_____

_____

Yes: _____
stand on His promises
_____

_____

Doodles & Notes

He makes all things beautiful in His time.

Jesus, I trust you with... _____

_____

_____

_____

_____

Handwritten Scripture

what I learned

⭐ armor check

the belt of truth – stand firm on what God says!

the breastplate of righteousness – holiness given/holiness lived.

the shoes of peace – stand firm, spread the news!

the shield of faith – be obedient in faith!

the helmet of salvation – take every thought captive.

the sword of the Spirit – learn to wield the Word of God.

On the third day, He
will come like rain.
Hosea 6:3

hymn or song:
_____
_____

◯ face-time with Jesus

(P)(R)_____
(A)(Y) & (P)(R)(A)(I)(S)(E)_____

(R)(E)_____
___(P)(E)_____
_____(N)(T) receive forgiveness
_____

(A)_____
___(S)_____
_____(K) He hears
_____

(Y)_____
___(E)_____
_____(S) Thank you, Jesus!
_____

HE MAKES BEAUTY FROM ASHES___ —>
JESUS, I TRUST YOU WITH:

_____
_____
_____
_____

Notes & Doodles

Handwritten Scripture

what I learned

armor check
the belt of truth - stand firm on what God says!
the breastplate of righteousness - holiness given/holiness lived.
the shoes of peace - stand firm, spread the news!
the shield of faith - be obedient in faith!
the helmet of salvation - take every thought captive.
the sword of the Spirit - learn to wield the Word of God.

This hope is a strong and trustworthy anchor for our souls. It leads us through the curtain into God's inner sanctuary.

Hebrews 6:19

hymn or song:

_____
_____
_____

☐ face-time with Jesus

Pray:
& Praise
_____
_____

Repent:
He gives grace
_____
_____

Ask:
& He will answer
_____
_____

Yes:
He will never leave you
_____
_____

Our struggle is not against flesh and blood.
Jesus, I trust you with:

Notes & Doodles

_____
_____
_____
_____
_____

Handwritten Scripture

_____

_____

_____

_____

_____

_____

_____

_____

_____

what I learned...

_____

_____

_____

_____

⭐ armor check

the belt of truth - stand firm on what God says!

the breastplate of righteousness - holiness given/holiness lived.

the shoes of peace - stand firm, spread the news!

the shield of faith - be obedient in faith!

the helmet of salvation - take every thought captive.

the sword of the Spirit - learn to wield the Word of God.

Grace received...Grace given.

_____

_____

_____

◯ **face-time with Jesus**

Pray: _____
   & Praise

_____

Repent: _____
He will come like the rain

_____

Ask: _____
let your request be known

_____

Yes: _____
He's a good Father

_____

Mercy Triumphs
JESUS, I TRUST YOU WITH:

_____

_____

_____

_____

Notes & Doodles

Handwritten Scripture

WHAT I LEARNED TODAY...

⊙ armor check
the belt of truth – stand firm on what God says!
the breastplate of righteousness – holiness given/holiness lived.
the shoes of peace – stand firm, spread the news!
the shield of faith – be obedient in faith!
the helmet of salvation – take every thought captive.
the sword of the Spirit – learn to wield the Word of God.

BLESSED IS SHE
WHOSE STRENGTH
IS THE LORD!

hymn or song:

_____

_____

face time with Jesus

Pray:
& Praise

_____

_____

Repent:
His blood covers it all

_____

_____

Ask:
and you will receive

_____

_____

Yes:
His blessings are amazing

_____

_____

Control is an illusion God has it.
Jesus, I trust you with:

_____

_____

_____

_____

_____

Notes & Doodles

Handwritten Scripture

_____
_____
_____
_____
_____
_____
_____
_____
_____
_____

what I learned

_____
_____
_____

◯ armor check

the belt of truth – stand firm on what God says!

the breastplate of righteousness – holiness given/holiness lived.

the shoes of peace – stand firm, spread the news!

the shield of faith – be obedient in faith!

the helmet of salvation – take every thought captive.

the sword of the Spirit – learn to wield the Word of God.

Hymn or Song _____

_____

→ face-time with Jesus

Pray:
& Praise
_____

_____

Repent:
strength is in forgiveness
_____

_____

Ask:
the Shepherd gives us what we need
_____

_____

Yes:
take Him at His Word
_____

_____

NOTES & DOODLES

Blessed is she whose strength is in the Lord.

Jesus, I trust you with...
Your grace is sufficient.

_____

_____

_____

_____

Handwritten Scripture

what I learned ———>

☐ ARMOR CHECK

the belt of truth - stand firm on what God says!

the breastplate of righteousness - holiness given/holiness lived.

the shoes of peace - stand firm, spread the news!

the shield of faith - be obedient in faith!

the helmet of salvation - take every thought captive.

the sword of the Spirit - learn to wield the Word of God.

Hymn or song _____

_____

_____

face-time with Jesus ⬅

Dare to live in the freedom Christ died to give you.

Pray: _____
& Praise _____

_____

Repent: _____
give it to Jesus _____

_____

Ask: _____
He is listening _____

_____

Yes: _____
His plan is good _____

_____

_____

He loves me, this I know.

JESUS, I TRUST YOU WITH... _____

_____

_____

_____

_____

Doodles & Notes

Handwritten Scripture

what I learned

⬭ armor check

the belt of truth – stand firm on what God says!

the breastplate of righteousness – holiness given/holiness lived.

the shoes of peace – stand firm, spread the news!

the shield of faith – be obedient in faith!

the helmet of salvation – take every thought captive.

the sword of the Spirit – learn to wield the Word of God.

Hymn or song _____

_____

_____

face-time with Jesus

Sadness to joy
Tiredness to dancing.
Sin-sick to healed.
All because of Jesus

Pray:
& Praise _____

_____

_____

Repent: _____
Create in me a clean heart!

_____

_____

Ask: _____
all I have needed, Your hand has provided

_____

_____

Yes: _____
Your Word is light to my path

_____

_____

notes & doodles

Jesus, I trust you with...
He is our peace.

_____

_____

_____

_____

_____

Handwritten Scripture

what I learned

☐ armor check

the belt of truth – stand firm on what God says!

the breastplate of righteousness – holiness given/holiness lived.

the shoes of peace – stand firm, spread the news!

the shield of faith – be obedient in faith!

the helmet of salvation – take every thought captive.

the sword of the Spirit – learn to wield the Word of God.

Hymn or song _____

_____

This is Your day, Lord, and I am Yours in it!

◯ face-time with Jesus

Pray:
& **Praise** _____

_____

Repent:
& He will give peace _____

_____

Ask:
pour out your heart _____

_____

Yes:
stand on His promises _____

_____

Doodles & Notes

He makes all things beautiful in His time.

Jesus, I trust you with... _____

_____

_____

_____

_____

Handwritten Scripture

_____

_____

_____

_____

_____

_____

_____

_____

_____

_____

_____

what I learned

_____

_____

_____

_____

☆ armor check

the belt of truth – stand firm on what God says!

the breastplate of righteousness – holiness given/holiness lived.

the shoes of peace – stand firm, spread the news!

the shield of faith – be obedient in faith!

the helmet of salvation – take every thought captive.

the sword of the Spirit – learn to wield the Word of God.

On the third day, He will come like rain.
Hosea 6:3

hymn or song:
_____
_____
_____

◯ face-time with Jesus

(P) (R)
(A)(Y) & (P)(R)(A)(I)(S)(E)
_____
_____

(R) (E)
    (P)(E)
       (N)(T) receive forgiveness
_____
_____

(A)
  (S)
   (K) He hears
_____
_____

(Y)
  (E)
   (S) Thank you, Jesus!
_____
_____

HE MAKES BEAUTY FROM ASHES
JESUS, I TRUST YOU WITH: —>

Notes & Doodles

_____

_____

_____

_____

Handwritten Scripture

▶ *what I learned*

armor check

the belt of truth — stand firm on what God says!

the breastplate of righteousness — holiness given/holiness lived.

the shoes of peace — stand firm, spread the news!

the shield of faith — be obedient in faith!

the helmet of salvation — take every thought captive.

the sword of the Spirit — learn to wield the Word of God.

This hope is a strong and trustworthy anchor for our souls. It leads us through the curtain into God's inner sanctuary.

Hebrews 6:19

hymn or song:

_____

_____

_____

☐ face-time with Jesus

Pray:
& Praise

_____

_____

Repent:
He gives grace

_____

_____

Ask:
& He will answer

_____

_____

Yes:
He will never leave you

_____

_____

Our struggle is not against flesh and blood.
Jesus, I trust you with:

_____

_____

_____

_____

_____

Notes & Doodles

Handwritten Scripture

what I learned...

☆ armor check

the belt of truth – stand firm on what God says!

the breastplate of righteousness – holiness given/holiness lived.

the shoes of peace – stand firm, spread the news!

the shield of faith – be obedient in faith!

the helmet of salvation – take every thought captive.

the sword of the Spirit – learn to wield the Word of God.

Grace received...Grace given.

○ **face-time with Jesus**

Pray:
& **P**raise

Repent:
He will come like the rain

Ask:
let your request be known

Yes:
He's a good Father

Mercy Triumphs
JESUS, I TRUST YOU WITH:

Notes & Doodles

Handwritten Scripture

What I Learned Today...

○ **armor check**
the belt of truth ~ stand firm on what God says!
the breastplate of righteousness ~ holiness given/holiness lived.
the shoes of peace ~ stand firm, spread the news!
the shield of faith ~ be obedient in faith!
the helmet of salvation ~ take every thought captive.
the sword of the Spirit ~ learn to wield the Word of God.

BLESSED IS SHE
WHOSE STRENGTH
IS THE LORD!

hymn or song:

_____

_____

face time with Jesus

Pray: _____
& Praise
_____

Repent: _____
His blood covers it all
_____

Ask: _____
and you will receive
_____

Yes: _____
His blessings are amazing
_____

Control is an illusion God has it.
Jesus, I trust you with:

_____

_____

_____

_____

Notes & Doodles

Handwritten Scripture

what I learned

◯armor check
the belt of truth – stand firm on what God says!
the breastplate of righteousness – holiness given/holiness lived.
the shoes of peace – stand firm, spread the news!
the shield of faith – be obedient in faith!
the helmet of salvation – take every thought captive.
the sword of the Spirit – learn to wield the Word of God.

Hymn or Song _____

_____

➡ face-time with Jesus

Pray: _____
& Praise _____

_____

Repent: _____
strength is in forgiveness _____

_____

Ask: _____
the Shepherd gives us what we need _____

_____

Yes: _____
take Him at His Word _____

_____

NOTES & DOODLES

Blessed is she
whose strength
is in the Lord.

Jesus, I trust you with...
Your grace is sufficient.

_____

_____

_____

_____

_____

Handwritten Scripture

_____
_____
_____
_____
_____
_____
_____
_____
_____
_____
_____

what I learned ⟶

_____
_____
_____
_____
_____

☐ ARMOR CHECK

the belt of truth – stand firm on what God says!

the breastplate of righteousness – holiness given/holiness lived.

the shoes of peace – stand firm, spread the news!

the shield of faith – be obedient in faith!

the helmet of salvation – take every thought captive.

the sword of the Spirit – learn to wield the Word of God.

Hymn or song _____

_____

face-time with Jesus ⬅

Dare to live in the freedom Christ died to give you.

Pray: _____
& Praise

_____

Repent: _____
give it to Jesus

_____

Ask: _____
He is listening

_____

Yes: _____
His plan is good

_____

_____

He loves me, this I know.

JESUS, I TRUST YOU WITH... _____

_____

_____

_____

_____

Doodles & Notes

Handwritten Scripture

what I learned

⬭ armor check

the belt of truth – stand firm on what God says!

the breastplate of righteousness – holiness given/holiness lived.

the shoes of peace – stand firm, spread the news!

the shield of faith – be obedient in faith!

the helmet of salvation – take every thought captive.

the sword of the Spirit – learn to wield the Word of God.

Hymn or song _____

_____

face-time with Jesus

Sadness to joy
Tiredness to dancing.
Sin-sick to healed.
All because of Jesus.

Pray:
& Praise _____

_____

Repent: _____
Create in me a clean heart!

_____

Ask: _____
all I have needed, Your hand has provided

_____

Yes: _____
Your Word is light to my path

_____

notes & doodles

Jesus, I trust you with...
He is our peace.

_____

_____

_____

_____

Handwritten Scripture

_____

_____

_____

_____

_____

_____

_____

_____

_____

_____

_____

what I learned

_____

_____

_____

☐ armor check

the belt of truth – stand firm on what God says!

the breastplate of righteousness – holiness given/holiness lived.

the shoes of peace – stand firm, spread the news!

the shield of faith – be obedient in faith!

the helmet of salvation – take every thought captive.

the sword of the Spirit – learn to wield the Word of God.

Hymn or song _____

_____

_____

○ face-time with Jesus

This is Your day, Lord, and I am Yours in it!

Pray:
& **Praise** _____

_____

_____

Repent:
& He will give peace _____

_____

_____

Ask:
pour out your heart _____

_____

_____

Yes:
stand on His promises _____

_____

_____

Doodles & Notes

He makes all things beautiful in His time.

Jesus, I trust you with...

_____

_____

_____

_____

Handwritten Scripture

what I learned

⭐ armor check

the belt of truth – stand firm on what God says!

the breastplate of righteousness – holiness given/holiness lived.

the shoes of peace – stand firm, spread the news!

the shield of faith – be obedient in faith!

the helmet of salvation – take every thought captive.

the sword of the Spirit – learn to wield the Word of God.

On the third day, He will come like rain.
Hosea 6:3

hymn or song:
_____

_____

◯ face-time with Jesus

P R _____
A Y & **P R A I S E**
_____

R E
P E _____
N T receive forgiveness
_____

A
S _____
K He hears
_____

Y
E _____
S Thank you, Jesus!
_____

HE makes BEAUTY from ashes ——>
JESUS, I TRUST YOU WITH:

Notes & Doodles

_____

_____

_____

_____

Handwritten Scripture

what I learned

armor check

the belt of truth — stand firm on what God says!

the breastplate of righteousness — holiness given/holiness lived.

the shoes of peace — stand firm, spread the news!

the shield of faith — be obedient in faith!

the helmet of salvation — take every thought captive.

the sword of the Spirit — learn to wield the Word of God.

This hope is a strong and trustworthy anchor for our souls. It leads us through the curtain into God's inner sanctuary.

Hebrews 6:19

hymn or song:
_____
_____

☐ face-time with Jesus

Pray:
& Praise
_____
_____

Repent:
He gives grace
_____
_____

Ask:
& He will answer
_____
_____

Yes:
He will never leave you
_____
_____

Our struggle is not against flesh and blood.

Jesus, I trust you with:

_____

Notes & Doodles

_____
_____
_____
_____

Handwritten Scripture

what I learned...

☆ armor check

the belt of truth – stand firm on what God says!

the breastplate of righteousness – holiness given/holiness lived.

the shoes of peace – stand firm, spread the news!

the shield of faith – be obedient in faith!

the helmet of salvation – take every thought captive.

the sword of the Spirit – learn to wield the Word of God.

Grace received...Grace given.

◯ **face-time with Jesus**

Pray:
& **P**raise

Repent:
He will come like the rain

Ask:
let your request be known

Yes:
He's a good Father

Mercy Triumphs
JESUS, I TRUST YOU WITH:

Notes & Doodles

Handwritten Scripture

What I Learned Today...

◯ armor check

the belt of truth ~ stand firm on what God says!

the breastplate of righteousness ~ holiness given/holiness lived.

the shoes of peace ~ stand firm, spread the news!

the shield of faith ~ be obedient in faith!

the helmet of salvation ~ take every thought captive.

the sword of the Spirit ~ learn to wield the Word of God.

BLESSED IS SHE
WHOSE STRENGTH
IS THE LORD!

hymn or song:

_____

_____

face-time with Jesus

Pray:
& Praise

_____

Repent: _____
His blood covers it all

_____

Ask: _____
and you will receive

_____

Yes: _____
His blessings are amazing

_____

Control is an illusion — God has it.
Jesus, I trust you with:

_____

_____

_____

_____

Notes & Doodles

Handwritten Scripture

_____

_____

_____

_____

_____

_____

_____

_____

_____

_____

what I learned

_____

_____

_____

_____

◯ armor check

the belt of truth – stand firm on what God says!

the breastplate of righteousness – holiness given/holiness lived.

the shoes of peace – stand firm, spread the news!

the shield of faith – be obedient in faith!

the helmet of salvation – take every thought captive.

the sword of the Spirit – learn to wield the Word of God.

Hymn or Song _____

_____

→ face-time with Jesus

Pray: _____

& Praise _____

Repent: _____

strength is in forgiveness

_____

Ask: _____

the Shepherd gives us what we need

_____

Yes: _____

take Him at His Word

_____

NOTES & DOODLES

Blessed is she
whose strength
is in the Lord.

Jesus, I trust you with...
Your grace is sufficient.

_____

_____

_____

_____

_____

Handwritten Scripture

what I learned ⟶

☐ ARMOR CHECK
the belt of truth – stand firm on what God says!
the breastplate of righteousness – holiness given/holiness lived.
the shoes of peace – stand firm, spread the news!
the shield of faith – be obedient in faith!
the helmet of salvation – take every thought captive.
the sword of the Spirit – learn to wield the Word of God.

Hymn or song _____

_____

_____

face-time with Jesus ⬅

Dare to live in the freedom Christ died to give you.

Pray: _____

& **Praise**

_____

Repent: _____

give it to Jesus

_____

Ask: _____

He is listening

_____

Yes: _____

His plan is good

_____

_____

He loves me, this I know.

JESUS, I TRUST YOU WITH... _____

_____

_____

_____

_____

Doodles & Notes

Handwritten Scripture

_____

_____

_____

_____

_____

_____

_____

_____

_____

_____

what I learned

_____

_____

_____

◯ armor check

the belt of truth - stand firm on what God says!

the breastplate of righteousness - holiness given/holiness lived.

the shoes of peace - stand firm, spread the news!

the shield of faith - be obedient in faith!

the helmet of salvation - take every thought captive.

the sword of the Spirit - learn to wield the Word of God.

Hymn or song _____

_____

_____

🍂 face-time with Jesus

Pray:
& Praise _____

_____

_____

Repent: _____
Create in me a clean heart!

_____

_____

Ask: _____
all I have needed, Your hand has provided

_____

_____

Yes: _____
Your Word is light to my path

_____

_____

notes & doodles

Sadness to joy
Tiredness to dancing.
Sin-sick to healed.
🌿 All because of Jesus. 🌿

Jesus, I trust you with...
He is our peace.

_____

_____

_____

_____

_____

Handwritten Scripture

what I learned

☐ armor check

the belt of truth – stand firm on what God says!

the breastplate of righteousness – holiness given/holiness lived.

the shoes of peace – stand firm, spread the news!

the shield of faith – be obedient in faith!

the helmet of salvation – take every thought captive.

the sword of the Spirit – learn to wield the Word of God.

Hymn or song _____

This is Your day, Lord, and I am Yours in it!

◯ face-time with Jesus

Pray: _____
 & Praise

Repent: _____
 & He will give peace

Ask: _____
 pour out your heart

Yes: _____
 stand on His promises

Doodles & Notes

He makes all things beautiful in His time.

Jesus, I trust you with...

Handwritten Scripture

_____
_____
_____
_____
_____
_____
_____
_____
_____
_____
_____
_____

what I learned

_____
_____
_____
_____

⭐ **armor check**

the belt of truth – stand firm on what God says!

the breastplate of righteousness – holiness given/holiness lived.

the shoes of peace – stand firm, spread the news!

the shield of faith – be obedient in faith!

the helmet of salvation – take every thought captive.

the sword of the Spirit – learn to wield the Word of God.

on the third day, He will come like rain.
Hosea 6:3

hymn or song:
_____

_____

_____

◯ face-time with Jesus

(P)(R)
(A)(Y) & (P)(R)(A)(I)(S)(E)
_____

(R)(E)
(P)(E)
(N)(T) receive forgiveness
_____

(A)
(S)
(K) He hears
_____

(Y)
(E)
(S) Thank you, Jesus!
_____

HE MAKES BEAUTY FROM ASHES ___ →
JESUS, I TRUST YOU WITH:

Notes & Doodles

_____
_____
_____
_____
_____

Handwritten Scripture

what I learned

armor check
the belt of truth – stand firm on what God says!

the breastplate of righteousness – holiness given/holiness lived.

the shoes of peace – stand firm, spread the news!

the shield of faith – be obedient in faith!

the helmet of salvation – take every thought captive.

the sword of the Spirit – learn to wield the Word of God.

This hope is a strong and trustworthy anchor for our souls. It leads us through the curtain into God's inner sanctuary.

Hebrews 6:19

hymn or song:

_____

_____

_____

▲ ☐ face-time with Jesus

Pray:
& Praise

_____

_____

Repent:
He gives grace

_____

_____

Ask:
& He will answer

_____

_____

Yes:
He will never leave you

_____

_____

Our struggle is not against flesh and blood.

Jesus, I trust you with:

Notes & Doodles

_____

_____

_____

_____

Handwritten Scripture

_____

_____

_____

_____

_____

_____

_____

_____

_____

what I learned...

_____

_____

_____

_____

☆ **armor check**

the belt of truth – stand firm on what God says!

the breastplate of righteousness – holiness given/holiness lived.

the shoes of peace – stand firm, spread the news!

the shield of faith – be obedient in faith!

the helmet of salvation – take every thought captive.

the sword of the Spirit – learn to wield the Word of God.

Grace received...Grace given.

hymn or song:

_____

_____

○ **face-time with Jesus**

Pray: _____
  & Praise _____

Repent: _____
He will come like the rain

_____

Ask: _____
let your request be known

_____

Yes: _____
He's a good Father

_____

Mercy Triumphs
JESUS, I TRUST YOU WITH:

▲ **Notes & Doodles**

_____

_____

_____

_____

_____

Handwritten Scripture

_____
_____
_____
_____
_____
_____
_____
_____
_____
_____
_____

WHaT I LearneD TODaY...

_____
_____
_____
_____

◯ armor check

the belt of truth ~ stand firm on what God says!
the breastplate of righteousness ~ holiness given/holiness
lived.
the shoes of peace ~ stand firm, spread the news!
the shield of faith ~ be obedient in faith!
the helmet of salvation ~ take every thought captive.
the sword of the Spirit ~ learn to wield the Word of God.

BLESSED IS SHE
WHOSE STRENGTH
IS THE LORD!

hymn or song:

_____

_____

face time with Jesus

Pray: _____
& Praise

_____

_____

Repent: _____
His blood covers it all

_____

_____

Ask: _____
and you will receive

_____

_____

Yes: _____
His blessings are amazing

_____

_____

Control is an illusion God has it.
Jesus, I trust you with:

_____

_____

_____

_____

_____

Notes & Doodles

Handwritten Scripture

_____

_____

_____

_____

_____

_____

_____

_____

_____

_____

what I learned

_____

_____

_____

_____

○ armor check
the belt of truth – stand firm on what God says!
the breastplate of righteousness – holiness given/holiness lived.
the shoes of peace – stand firm, spread the news!
the shield of faith – be obedient in faith!
the helmet of salvation – take every thought captive.
the sword of the Spirit – learn to wield the Word of God.

Hymn or Song _____

_____

→ face-time with Jesus

Pray: _____
& Praise _____

_____

Repent: _____
strength is in forgiveness

_____

Ask: _____
the Shepherd gives us what we need

_____

Yes: _____
take Him at His Word

_____

NOTES & DOODLES

Blessed is she
whose strength
is in the Lord.

Jesus, I trust you with...
Your grace is sufficient.

_____

_____

_____

_____

Handwritten Scripture

_what I learned ___→

☐ ARMOR CHECK
the belt of truth – stand firm on what God says!
the breastplate of righteousness – holiness given/holiness lived.
the shoes of peace – stand firm, spread the news!
the shield of faith – be obedient in faith!
the helmet of salvation – take every thought captive.
the sword of the Spirit – learn to wield the Word of God.

Hymn or song

_____

_____

face-time with Jesus ⬅

Dare to live in the freedom Christ died to give you.

Pray:
& Praise

_____

Repent:
give it to Jesus

_____

Ask:
He is listening

_____

Yes:
His plan is good

_____

_____

He loves me, this I know.

Doodles & Notes

JESUS, I TRUST YOU WITH...

_____

_____

_____

_____

Handwritten Scripture

_____

_____

_____

_____

_____

_____

_____

_____

_____

_____

what I learned

_____

_____

_____

_____

⬭ armor check
the belt of truth – stand firm on what God says!

the breastplate of righteousness – holiness given/holiness lived.

the shoes of peace – stand firm, spread the news!

the shield of faith – be obedient in faith!

the helmet of salvation – take every thought captive.

the sword of the Spirit – learn to wield the Word of God.

Hymn or song _____

_____

face-time with Jesus

Sadness to joy
Tiredness to dancing.
Sin-sick to healed.
All because of Jesus

Pray: _____
& Praise _____

_____

Repent: _____
Create in me a clean heart!

_____

_____

Ask: _____
all I have needed, Your hand has provided

_____

_____

Yes: _____
Your Word is light to my path

_____

notes & doodles

Jesus, I trust you with...
He is our peace.

_____

_____

_____

_____

_____

Handwritten Scripture

_____

_____

_____

_____

_____

_____

_____

_____

_____

_____

_____

what I learned

_____

_____

_____

_____

☐ armor check

the belt of truth – stand firm on what God says!

the breastplate of righteousness – holiness given/holiness lived.

the shoes of peace – stand firm, spread the news!

the shield of faith – be obedient in faith!

the helmet of salvation – take every thought captive.

the sword of the Spirit – learn to wield the Word of God.

Hymn or song _____

_____

_____

This is Your day, Lord, and I am Yours in it!

○ face-time with Jesus

Pray:
& Praise

_____

_____

Repent:
& He will give peace

_____

_____

Ask:
pour out your heart

_____

_____

Yes:
stand on His promises

_____

_____

Doodles & Notes

He makes all things beautiful in His time.

Jesus, I trust you with...

_____

_____

_____

_____

Handwritten Scripture

what I learned

⭐ armor check

the belt of truth – stand firm on what God says!
the breastplate of righteousness – holiness given/holiness lived.
the shoes of peace – stand firm, spread the news!
the shield of faith – be obedient in faith!
the helmet of salvation – take every thought captive.
the sword of the Spirit – learn to wield the Word of God.

on the third day, He will come like rain.
Hosea 6:3

◯ face-time with Jesus

(P)(R)
(A)(Y) & (P)(R)(A)(I)(S)(E)

(R)(E)
(P)(E)
(N)(T) receive forgiveness

(A)
(S)
(K) He hears

(Y)
(E)
(S) Thank you, Jesus!

He makes beauty from ashes —>
JESUS, I TRUST YOU WITH:

Notes & Doodles

Handwritten Scripture

what I learned

armor check

the belt of truth – stand firm on what God says!

the breastplate of righteousness – holiness given/holiness lived.

the shoes of peace – stand firm, spread the news!

the shield of faith – be obedient in faith!

the helmet of salvation – take every thought captive.

the sword of the Spirit – learn to wield the Word of God.

This hope is a strong and trustworthy anchor for our souls. It leads us through the curtain into God's inner sanctuary.

Hebrews 6:19

hymn or song:

_____

_____

_____

☐ face-time with Jesus

Pray:
& Praise

_____

_____

Repent:
He gives grace

_____

_____

Ask:
& He will answer

_____

_____

Yes:
He will never leave you

_____

_____

Our struggle is not against flesh and blood.

Jesus, I trust you with:

Notes & Doodles

_____

_____

_____

_____

Handwritten Scripture

what I learned...

☆ armor check
the belt of truth – stand firm on what God says!
the breastplate of righteousness – holiness given/holiness lived.
the shoes of peace – stand firm, spread the news!
the shield of faith – be obedient in faith!
the helmet of salvation – take every thought captive.
the sword of the Spirit – learn to wield the Word of God.

Grace received...Grace given.

_____

_____

◯ **face-time with Jesus**

Pray: _____
    & **P**raise
_____

Repent: _____
He will come like the rain
_____

Ask: _____
let your request be known
_____

Yes: _____
He's a good Father
_____

Mercy Triumphs
JESUS, I TRUST YOU WITH:

Notes & Doodles

_____

_____

_____

_____

_____

Handwritten Scripture

WHaT I LearneD ToDay...

◯ armor check
the belt of truth – stand firm on what God says!
the breastplate of righteousness – holiness given/holiness
lived.
the shoes of peace – stand firm, spread the news!
the shield of faith – be obedient in faith!
the helmet of salvation – take every thought captive.
the sword of the Spirit – learn to wield the Word of God.

BLESSED IS SHE
WHOSE STRENGTH
IS THE LORD!

hymn or song:

face-time with Jesus

Pray:
& Praise

Repent:
His blood covers it all

Ask:
and you will receive

Yes:
His blessings are amazing

Control is an illusion God has it.
Jesus, I trust you with:

Notes & Doodles

Handwritten Scripture

_____

_____

_____

_____

_____

_____

_____

_____

_____

what I learned

_____

_____

_____

_____

◯ armor check

the belt of truth – stand firm on what God says!

the breastplate of righteousness – holiness given/holiness lived.

the shoes of peace – stand firm, spread the news!

the shield of faith – be obedient in faith!

the helmet of salvation – take every thought captive.

the sword of the Spirit – learn to wield the Word of God.

Hymn or Song _____

_____

➡ face-time with Jesus

Blessed is she whose strength is in the Lord.

Pray: _____
& Praise _____

Repent: _____
strength is in forgiveness _____

Ask: _____
the Shepherd gives us what we need _____

Yes: _____
take Him at His Word _____

notes & doodles

Jesus, I trust you with...
Your grace is sufficient.

_____

_____

_____

_____

Handwritten Scripture

what I learned ⟶

☐ ARMOR CHECK

the belt of truth – stand firm on what God says!

the breastplate of righteousness – holiness given/holiness lived.

the shoes of peace – stand firm, spread the news!

the shield of faith – be obedient in faith!

the helmet of salvation – take every thought captive.

the sword of the Spirit – learn to wield the Word of God.

Hymn or song _____

_____

_____

face-time with Jesus ⬅

Dare to live in the freedom Christ died to give you.

Pray: _____

& Praise

_____

_____

Repent: _____

give it to Jesus

_____

_____

Ask: _____

He is listening

_____

_____

Yes: _____

His plan is good

_____

_____

He loves me, this I know.

JESUS, I TRUST YOU WITH...

_____

_____

_____

_____

Doodles & Notes

Handwritten Scripture

what I learned

◯ armor check
the belt of truth – stand firm on what God says!
the breastplate of righteousness – holiness given/holiness lived.
the shoes of peace – stand firm, spread the news!
the shield of faith – be obedient in faith!
the helmet of salvation – take every thought captive.
the sword of the Spirit – learn to wield the Word of God.

Hymn or song _____

_____

face-time with Jesus

Pray: _____
& Praise
_____

Repent: _____
Create in me a clean heart!
_____

Ask: _____
all I have needed, Your hand has provided
_____

Yes: _____
Your Word is light to my path
_____

notes & doodles

Sadness to joy
Tiredness to dancing.
Sin-sick to healed.
All because of Jesus.

Jesus, I trust you with...
He is our peace.

_____

_____

_____

_____

_____

Handwritten Scripture

_____
_____
_____
_____
_____
_____
_____
_____
_____
_____
_____
_____

what I learned

_____
_____
_____
_____

☐ armor check
the belt of truth – stand firm on what God says!
the breastplate of righteousness – holiness given/holiness lived.
the shoes of peace – stand firm, spread the news!
the shield of faith – be obedient in faith!
the helmet of salvation – take every thought captive.
the sword of the Spirit – learn to wield the Word of God.

Hymn or song _____

_____

_____

This is Your day, lord, and I am Yours in it!

◯ face-time with Jesus

Pray:
& Praise _____

_____

Repent:
& He will give peace _____

_____

Ask:
pour out your heart _____

_____

Yes:
stand on His promises _____

_____

Doodles & Notes

He makes all things beautiful in His time.

Jesus, I trust you with...

_____

_____

_____

_____

Handwritten Scripture

_____
_____
_____
_____
_____
_____
_____
_____
_____
_____
_____

what I learned

_____
_____
_____
_____

☆ armor check

the belt of truth – stand firm on what God says!

the breastplate of righteousness – holiness given/holiness lived.

the shoes of peace – stand firm, spread the news!

the shield of faith – be obedient in faith!

the helmet of salvation – take every thought captive.

the sword of the Spirit – learn to wield the Word of God.

On the third day, He will come like rain.
Hosea 6:3

hymn or song:

_____

_____

○ face-time with Jesus

P R
A Y & **P R A I S E**

R E
P E
N T receive forgiveness

A
S
K He hears

Y
E
S Thank you, Jesus!

HE MAKES BEAUTY FROM ASHES ——→
JESUS, I TRUST YOU WITH:

Notes & Doodles

Handwritten Scripture

what I learned

armor check

the belt of truth – stand firm on what God says!

the breastplate of righteousness – holiness given/holiness lived.

the shoes of peace – stand firm, spread the news!

the shield of faith – be obedient in faith!

the helmet of salvation – take every thought captive.

the sword of the Spirit – learn to wield the Word of God.

This hope is a strong and trustworthy anchor for our souls. It leads us through the curtain into God's inner sanctuary.

Hebrews 6:19

hymn or song:

_____

_____

_____

☐ face-time with Jesus

Pray:
& Praise

_____

_____

Repent:
He gives grace

_____

_____

Ask:
& He will answer

_____

_____

Yes:
He will never leave you

_____

_____

Our struggle is not against flesh and blood.

Jesus, I trust you with:

_____

_____

_____

_____

Notes & Doodles

Handwritten Scripture

what I learned...

the belt of truth – stand firm on what God says!

the breastplate of righteousness – holiness given/holiness lived.

the shoes of peace – stand firm, spread the news!

the shield of faith – be obedient in faith!

the helmet of salvation – take every thought captive.

the sword of the Spirit – learn to wield the Word of God.

Grace received...Grace given.

_____

_____

○ **face-time with Jesus**

Pray: _____
& Praise

_____

Repent: _____
He will come like the rain

_____

Ask: _____
let your request be known

_____

Yes: _____
He's a good Father

_____

Mercy Triumphs
JESUS, I TRUST YOU WITH:

_____

_____

_____

_____

_____

Notes & Doodles

Handwritten Scripture

_____

_____

_____

_____

_____

_____

_____

_____

_____

_____

WHAT I LEARNED TODAY...

_____

_____

_____

armor check

the belt of truth ~ stand firm on what God says!
the breastplate of righteousness ~ holiness given/holiness
lived.
the shoes of peace ~ stand firm, spread the news!
the shield of faith ~ be obedient in faith!
the helmet of salvation ~ take every thought captive.
the sword of the Spirit ~ learn to wield the Word of God.

BLESSED IS SHE
WHOSE STRENGTH
IS THE LORD!

hymn or song:

face-time with Jesus

Pray:
& Praise

Repent:
His blood covers it all

Ask:
and you will receive

Yes:
His blessings are amazing

Control is an illusion God has it.
Jesus, I trust you with:

Notes & Doodles

Handwritten Scripture

what I learned

◯ armor check
the belt of truth – stand firm on what God says!
the breastplate of righteousness – holiness given/holiness lived.
the shoes of peace – stand firm, spread the news!
the shield of faith – be obedient in faith!
the helmet of salvation – take every thought captive.
the sword of the Spirit – learn to wield the Word of God.

Hymn or Song _____

_____

➜ face-time with Jesus

Pray: _____

& Praise _____

_____

Repent: _____
strength is in forgiveness

_____

Ask: _____
the Shepherd gives us what we need

_____

Yes: _____
take Him at His Word

_____

NOTES & DOODLES

Blessed is she
whose strength
is in the Lord.

Jesus, I trust you with...
Your grace is sufficient.

_____

_____

_____

_____

_____

Handwritten Scripture

_____
_____
_____
_____
_____
_____
_____
_____
_____
_____

what I learned →

_____
_____
_____
_____

☐ ARMOR CHECK

the belt of truth - stand firm on what God says!
the breastplate of righteousness - holiness given/holiness lived.
the shoes of peace - stand firm, spread the news!
the shield of faith - be obedient in faith!
the helmet of salvation - take every thought captive.
the sword of the Spirit - learn to wield the Word of God.

Hymn or song _____

_____

_____

face-time with Jesus ⇦

Dare to live in the freedom Christ died to give you...

Pray:
& Praise
_____

_____

Repent:
give it to Jesus
_____

_____

Ask:
He is listening
_____

_____

Yes:
His plan is good
_____

_____

_____

He loves me, this I know.

JESUS, I TRUST YOU WITH...

_____

_____

_____

_____

Doodles & Notes

Handwritten Scripture

what I learned

○ **armor check**

the belt of truth – stand firm on what God says!

the breastplate of righteousness – holiness given/holiness lived.

the shoes of peace – stand firm, spread the news!

the shield of faith – be obedient in faith!

the helmet of salvation – take every thought captive.

the sword of the Spirit – learn to wield the Word of God.

Hymn or song

_____

_____

Sadness to joy
Tiredness to dancing.
Sin-sick to healed.
All because of Jesus.

face-time with Jesus

Pray: _____
& Praise
_____

Repent: _____
Create in me a clean heart!
_____

Ask: _____
all I have needed, Your hand has provided
_____

Yes: _____
Your Word is light to my path
_____

notes & doodles

Jesus, I trust you with...
He is our peace.

_____

_____

_____

_____

Handwritten Scripture

_____
_____
_____
_____
_____
_____
_____
_____
_____
_____
_____
_____

what I learned

_____
_____
_____
_____

☐ armor check

the belt of truth – stand firm on what God says!

the breastplate of righteousness – holiness given/holiness lived.

the shoes of peace – stand firm, spread the news!

the shield of faith – be obedient in faith!

the helmet of salvation – take every thought captive.

the sword of the Spirit – learn to wield the Word of God.

Hymn or song _____

_____

_____

This is Your day, Lord, and I am Yours in it!

◯ face-time with Jesus

Pray:
& Praise

_____

_____

Repent:
& He will give peace

_____

_____

Ask:
pour out your heart

_____

_____

Yes:
stand on His promises

_____

_____

Doodles & Notes

He makes all things beautiful in His time.

Jesus, I trust you with...

_____

_____

_____

_____

Handwritten Scripture

_____

_____

_____

_____

_____

_____

_____

_____

_____

_____

_____

what I learned

_____

_____

_____

☆ armor check

the belt of truth – stand firm on what God says!

the breastplate of righteousness – holiness given/holiness lived.

the shoes of peace – stand firm, spread the news!

the shield of faith – be obedient in faith!

the helmet of salvation – take every thought captive.

the sword of the Spirit – learn to wield the Word of God.

On the third day, He will come like rain.
Hosea 6:3

hymn or song:
_____
_____
_____

◯ face-time with Jesus

P R A Y & P R A I S E
_____
_____

R E P E N T receive forgiveness
_____
_____

A S K He hears
_____
_____

Y E S Thank you, Jesus!
_____
_____

HE MAKES BEAUTY FROM ASHES
JESUS, I TRUST YOU WITH: ——>

Notes & Doodles

_____
_____
_____
_____
_____

Handwritten Scripture

▶ what I learned

◯ armor check

the belt of truth – stand firm on what God says!

the breastplate of righteousness – holiness given/holiness lived.

the shoes of peace – stand firm, spread the news!

the shield of faith – be obedient in faith!

the helmet of salvation – take every thought captive.

the sword of the Spirit – learn to wield the Word of God.

This hope is a strong and trustworthy anchor for our souls. It leads us through the curtain into God's inner sanctuary.

Hebrews 6:19

hymn or song:

_____

_____

_____

☐ face-time with Jesus

Pray:
& Praise

_____

_____

Repent:
He gives grace

_____

_____

Ask:
& He will answer

_____

_____

Yes:
He will never leave you

_____

_____

Our struggle is not against flesh and blood.

Jesus, I trust you with:

_____

_____

_____

_____

Notes & Doodles

Handwritten Scripture

_____

_____

_____

_____

_____

_____

_____

_____

_____

_____

what I learned...

_____

_____

_____

_____

⭐ armor check

the belt of truth – stand firm on what God says!

the breastplate of righteousness – holiness given/holiness lived.

the shoes of peace – stand firm, spread the news!

the shield of faith – be obedient in faith!

the helmet of salvation – take every thought captive.

the sword of the Spirit – learn to wield the Word of God.

Grace received...Grace given.

⭕ **face-time with Jesus**

Pray:
& Praise

Repent:
He will come like the rain

Ask:
let your request be known

Yes:
He's a good Father

Mercy Triumphs
JESUS, I TRUST YOU WITH:

◄ **Notes & Doodles**

Handwritten Scripture

What I Learned Today...

◯ armor check

the belt of truth – stand firm on what God says!

the breastplate of righteousness – holiness given/holiness lived.

the shoes of peace – stand firm, spread the news!

the shield of faith – be obedient in faith!

the helmet of salvation – take every thought captive.

the sword of the Spirit – learn to wield the Word of God.

BLESSED IS SHE
WHOSE STRENGTH
IS THE LORD!

hymn or song:

_____

_____

face-time with Jesus

Pray: _____
& Praise

_____

Repent: _____
His blood covers it all

_____

Ask: _____
and you will receive

_____

Yes: _____
His blessings are amazing

_____

Control is an illusion God has it.
Jesus, I trust you with:

_____

_____

_____

_____

Notes & Doodles

Handwritten Scripture

what I learned

⭕ armor check

the belt of truth – stand firm on what God says!

the breastplate of righteousness – holiness given/holiness lived.

the shoes of peace – stand firm, spread the news!

the shield of faith – be obedient in faith!

the helmet of salvation – take every thought captive.

the sword of the Spirit – learn to wield the Word of God.

Hymn or Song

_____

_____

→ face-time with Jesus

Blessed is she whose strength is in the Lord.

Pray: _____
& Praise _____

Repent: _____
strength is in forgiveness

_____

Ask: _____
the Shepherd gives us what we need

_____

Yes: _____
take Him at His Word

_____

_____

NOTES & DOODLES

Jesus, I trust you with...
Your grace is sufficient.

_____

_____

_____

_____

_____

Handwritten Scripture

_____

_____

_____

_____

_____

_____

_____

_____

_____

_____

what I learned ⟶

_____

_____

_____

_____

☐ ARMOR CHECK

the belt of truth – stand firm on what God says!

the breastplate of righteousness – holiness given/holiness lived.

the shoes of peace – stand firm, spread the news!

the shield of faith – be obedient in faith!

the helmet of salvation – take every thought captive.

the sword of the Spirit – learn to wield the Word of God.

Hymn or song _____

_____

_____

face-time with Jesus ⬅

Dare to live in the
freedom Christ
died to give you.

Pray: _____
& Praise
_____

Repent: _____
give it to Jesus
_____

_____

Ask: _____
He is listening
_____

_____

Yes: _____
His plan is good
_____

_____

He loves me, this I know.

JESUS, I TRUST YOU WITH...
_____

_____

_____

_____

_____

Doodles & Notes

Handwritten Scripture

_____
_____
_____
_____
_____
_____
_____
_____
_____
_____

what I learned

_____
_____
_____
_____

◯ armor check

the belt of truth – stand firm on what God says!

the breastplate of righteousness – holiness given/holiness lived.

the shoes of peace – stand firm, spread the news!

the shield of faith – be obedient in faith!

the helmet of salvation – take every thought captive.

the sword of the Spirit – learn to wield the Word of God.

Hymn or song
_____

_____

face-time with Jesus

Sadness to joy
Tiredness to dancing.
Sin-sick to healed.
All because of Jesus.

Pray:
& Praise
_____

_____

Repent:
Create in me a clean heart!
_____

_____

Ask:
all I have needed, Your hand has provided
_____

_____

Yes:
Your Word is light to my path
_____

notes & doodles

Jesus, I trust you with...
He is our peace.
_____

_____

_____

_____

_____

Handwritten Scripture

what I learned

☐ armor check

the belt of truth – stand firm on what God says!

the breastplate of righteousness – holiness given/holiness lived.

the shoes of peace – stand firm, spread the news!

the shield of faith – be obedient in faith!

the helmet of salvation – take every thought captive.

the sword of the Spirit – learn to wield the Word of God.

Hymn or song _____

_____

_____

This is your day, lord, and I am yours in it!

◯ face-time with Jesus

Pray:
& Praise _____

_____

Repent:
& He will give peace _____

_____

Ask:
pour out your heart _____

_____

Yes:
stand on His promises _____

_____

Doodles & Notes

He makes all things beautiful in His time.

Jesus, I trust you with... _____

_____

_____

_____

_____

Handwritten Scripture

what I learned

⭐ armor check

the belt of truth – stand firm on what God says!

the breastplate of righteousness – holiness given/holiness lived.

the shoes of peace – stand firm, spread the news!

the shield of faith – be obedient in faith!

the helmet of salvation – take every thought captive.

the sword of the Spirit – learn to wield the Word of God.

On the third day, He
will come like rain.
Hosea 6:3

hymn or song:
_____

_____

◯ face-time with Jesus

P R
A Y & P R A I S E
_____

R E
P E
N T receive forgiveness
_____

A
S
K He hears
_____

Y
E
S Thank you, Jesus!
_____

He makes beauty from ashes ——→
JESUS, I TRUST YOU WITH:

Notes & Doodles

Handwritten Scripture

_____
_____
_____
_____
_____
_____
_____
_____
_____
_____

► what I learned

_____
_____
_____
_____
_____

◯ armor check

the belt of truth – stand firm on what God says!

the breastplate of righteousness – holiness given/holiness lived.

the shoes of peace – stand firm, spread the news!

the shield of faith – be obedient in faith!

the helmet of salvation – take every thought captive.

the sword of the Spirit – learn to wield the Word of God.

This hope is a strong and trustworthy anchor for our souls. It leads us through the curtain into God's inner sanctuary.

Hebrews 6:19

hymn or song:

_____

_____

☐ face-time with Jesus

Pray:
& Praise

_____

Repent:
He gives grace

_____

Ask:
& He will answer

_____

Yes:
He will never leave you

_____

Our struggle is not against flesh and blood.
Jesus, I trust you with:

Notes & Doodles

_____

_____

_____

_____

Handwritten Scripture

_____

_____

_____

_____

_____

_____

_____

_____

_____

_____

what I learned...

_____

_____

_____

☆ armor check

the belt of truth – stand firm on what God says!

the breastplate of righteousness – holiness given/holiness lived.

the shoes of peace – stand firm, spread the news!

the shield of faith – be obedient in faith!

the helmet of salvation – take every thought captive.

the sword of the Spirit – learn to wield the Word of God.

Grace received...Grace given.

hymn or song:

_____
_____
_____

◯ face-time with Jesus

Pray: _____
& Praise
_____

Repent: _____
He will come like the rain
_____

Ask: _____
let your request be known
_____

Yes: _____
He's a good Father
_____

Mercy Triumphs
JESUS, I TRUST YOU WITH:

◄ ◄ **Notes & Doodles**

_____
_____
_____
_____
_____

Handwritten Scripture

_____

What I Learned Today...

◯ armor check
the belt of truth – stand firm on what God says!
the breastplate of righteousness – holiness given/holiness
lived.
the shoes of peace – stand firm, spread the news!
the shield of faith – be obedient in faith!
the helmet of salvation – take every thought captive.
the sword of the Spirit – learn to wield the Word of God.

BLESSED IS SHE
WHOSE STRENGTH
IS THE LORD!

hymn or song:

_____

_____

face time with Jesus

Pray: _____
& Praise

_____

Repent: _____
His blood covers it all

_____

Ask: _____
and you will receive

_____

Yes: _____
His blessings are amazing

_____

Control is an illusion ▸ God has it.
Jesus, I trust you with:

Notes & Doodles

_____

_____

_____

_____

Handwritten Scripture

_____

_____

_____

_____

_____

_____

_____

_____

_____

_____

what I learned

_____

_____

_____

◯ armor check

the belt of truth – stand firm on what God says!

the breastplate of righteousness – holiness given/holiness lived.

the shoes of peace – stand firm, spread the news!

the shield of faith – be obedient in faith!

the helmet of salvation – take every thought captive.

the sword of the Spirit – learn to wield the Word of God.

Hymn or Song _____

_____

➡ face-time with Jesus

Blessed is she whose strength is in the Lord.

Pray: _____
& Praise

_____

Repent: _____
strength is in forgiveness

_____

Ask: _____
the Shepherd gives us what we need

_____

Yes: _____
take Him at His Word

_____

NOTES & DOODLES

Jesus, I trust you with...
Your grace is sufficient.

_____

_____

_____

_____

_____

Handwritten Scripture

what I learned ⟶

☐ ARMOR CHECK

the belt of truth – stand firm on what God says!

the breastplate of righteousness – holiness given/holiness lived.

the shoes of peace – stand firm, spread the news!

the shield of faith – be obedient in faith!

the helmet of salvation – take every thought captive.

the sword of the Spirit – learn to wield the Word of God.

HYMN or song _____

_____

_____

face-time with Jesus ⬅

Dare to live in the freedom Christ died to give you.

Pray: _____

& Praise _____

Repent: _____

give it to Jesus _____

Ask: _____

He is listening _____

Yes: _____

His plan is good _____

_____

He loves me, this I know.

JESUS, I TRUST YOU WITH... _____

_____

_____

_____

Doodles & Notes

Handwritten Scripture

what I learned

armor check

the belt of truth – stand firm on what God says!

the breastplate of righteousness – holiness given/holiness lived.

the shoes of peace – stand firm, spread the news!

the shield of faith – be obedient in faith!

the helmet of salvation – take every thought captive.

the sword of the Spirit – learn to wield the Word of God.

Hymn or song
_____
_____

face-time with Jesus

Sadness to joy
Tiredness to dancing.
Sin-sick to healed.
All because of Jesus.

Pray:
& Praise _____
_____
_____

Repent: _____
Create in me a clean heart!
_____
_____

Ask: _____
all I have needed, Your hand has provided
_____
_____

Yes: _____
Your Word is light to my path
_____

notes & doodles

Jesus, I trust you with...
He is our peace.
_____
_____
_____
_____
_____

Handwritten Scripture

what I learned

☐ armor check

the belt of truth – stand firm on what God says!
the breastplate of righteousness – holiness given/holiness lived.
the shoes of peace – stand firm, spread the news!
the shield of faith – be obedient in faith!
the helmet of salvation – take every thought captive.
the sword of the Spirit – learn to wield the Word of God.

Hymn or song _____

_____

_____

This is Your day, lord, and I am yours in it!

◯ face-time with Jesus

Pray:
& Praise
_____

_____

Repent:
& He will give peace

_____

_____

Ask:
pour out your heart

_____

_____

Yes:
stand on His promises

_____

_____

Doodles & Notes

He makes all things beautiful in His time.

Jesus, I trust you with... _____

_____

_____

_____

_____

Handwritten Scripture

_____
_____
_____
_____
_____
_____
_____
_____
_____
_____
_____

what I learned

_____
_____
_____
_____

☆ **armor check**

the belt of truth – stand firm on what God says!
the breastplate of righteousness – holiness given/holiness lived.
the shoes of peace – stand firm, spread the news!
the shield of faith – be obedient in faith!
the helmet of salvation – take every thought captive.
the sword of the Spirit – learn to wield the Word of God.

On the third day, He will come like rain.
Hosea 6:3

hymn or song:
_____
_____
_____

◯ face-time with Jesus

P R A Y & P R A I S E
_____
_____

R E P E N T receive forgiveness
_____
_____

A S K He hears
_____
_____

Y E S Thank you, Jesus!
_____
_____

He makes beauty from ashes
JESUS, I TRUST YOU WITH: ——>

Notes & Doodles

_____
_____
_____
_____

Handwritten Scripture

what I learned

⃝ armor check

the belt of truth – stand firm on what God says!

the breastplate of righteousness – holiness given/holiness lived.

the shoes of peace – stand firm, spread the news!

the shield of faith – be obedient in faith!

the helmet of salvation – take every thought captive.

the sword of the Spirit – learn to wield the Word of God.

This hope is a strong and trustworthy anchor for our souls. It leads us through the curtain into God's inner sanctuary.
Hebrews 6:19

hymn or song:
_____
_____
_____

▲ ☐ face-time with Jesus

Pray:
& Praise
_____
_____

Repent:
He gives grace
_____
_____

Ask:
& He will answer
_____
_____

Yes:
He will never leave you
_____
_____

Our struggle is not against flesh and blood.
Jesus, I trust you with:

Notes & Doodles

_____
_____
_____
_____
_____

Handwritten Scripture

what I learned...

⭐ armor check

the belt of truth – stand firm on what God says!

the breastplate of righteousness – holiness given/holiness lived.

the shoes of peace – stand firm, spread the news!

the shield of faith – be obedient in faith!

the helmet of salvation – take every thought captive.

the sword of the Spirit – learn to wield the Word of God.

Grace received...Grace given.

_____
_____

◯ **face-time with Jesus**

Pray:
& **P**raise
_____
_____

Repent:_____
He will come like the rain
_____

Ask: _____
let your request be known
_____

Yes: _____
He's a good Father
_____

_____
Mercy Triumphs
JESUS, I TRUST YOU WITH:

Notes & Doodles

_____
_____
_____
_____
_____

Handwritten Scripture

_____

_____

_____

_____

_____

_____

_____

_____

_____

WHaT I LearneD TODaY...

_____

_____

_____

_____

◯ armor check

the belt of truth ~ stand firm on what God says!
the breastplate of righteousness ~ holiness given/holiness lived.
the shoes of peace ~ stand firm, spread the news!
the shield of faith ~ be obedient in faith!
the helmet of salvation ~ take every thought captive.
the sword of the Spirit ~ learn to wield the Word of God.

BLESSED IS SHE
WHOSE STRENGTH
IS THE LORD!

hymn or song:

_____

_____

face-time with Jesus

Pray: _____
& Praise

Repent: _____
His blood covers it all

Ask: _____
and you will receive

Yes: _____
His blessings are amazing

Control is an illusion > God has it.
Jesus, I trust you with:

_____

_____

_____

_____

Notes & Doodles

Handwritten Scripture

what I learned

⊃armor check

the belt of truth – stand firm on what God says!

the breastplate of righteousness – holiness given/holiness lived.

the shoes of peace – stand firm, spread the news!

the shield of faith – be obedient in faith!

the helmet of salvation – take every thought captive.

the sword of the Spirit – learn to wield the Word of God.

Hymn or Song _____

_____

➡ face-time with Jesus

Pray: _____

& Praise

_____

Repent: _____

strength is in forgiveness

_____

Ask: _____

the Shepherd gives us what we need

_____

Yes: _____

take Him at His Word

_____

Blessed is she whose strength is in the Lord.

NOTES & DOODLES

Jesus, I trust you with...
Your grace is sufficient.

_____

_____

_____

_____

Handwritten Scripture

_____

_____

_____

_____

_____

_____

_____

_____

_____

_____

_____

what I learned ⟶ _____

_____

_____

_____

_____

☐ ARMOR CHECK

the belt of truth – stand firm on what God says!

the breastplate of righteousness – holiness given/holiness lived.

the shoes of peace – stand firm, spread the news!

the shield of faith – be obedient in faith!

the helmet of salvation – take every thought captive.

the sword of the Spirit – learn to wield the Word of God.

HYMN OF SONG _____

_____

_____

face-time with Jesus ⬅

Dare to live in the
freedom Christ
died to give you.

Pray: _____
& **Praise** _____

Repent: _____
give it to Jesus _____

Ask: _____
He is listening _____

Yes: _____
His plan is good _____

_____

He loves me, this I know.

JESUS, I TRUST YOU WITH...
_____

_____

_____

_____

Doodles & Notes

Handwritten Scripture

_____

_____

_____

_____

_____

_____

_____

_____

_____

_____

what I learned

_____

_____

_____

_____

◯ armor check

the belt of truth – stand firm on what God says!

the breastplate of righteousness – holiness given/holiness lived.

the shoes of peace – stand firm, spread the news!

the shield of faith – be obedient in faith!

the helmet of salvation – take every thought captive.

the sword of the Spirit – learn to wield the Word of God.

HYMN or song _____

_____

_____

face-time with Jesus

Sadness to joy
Tiredness to dancing.
Sin-sick to healed.
All because of Jesus.

Pray: _____
& *Praise*
_____

Repent: _____
Create in me a clean heart!

_____

Ask: _____
all I have needed, Your hand has provided

_____

Yes: _____
Your Word is light to my path

_____

notes & doodles

Jesus, I trust you with...
He is our peace.

_____

_____

_____

_____

_____

Handwritten Scripture

what I learned

☐ armor check

the belt of truth – stand firm on what God says!

the breastplate of righteousness – holiness given/holiness lived.

the shoes of peace – stand firm, spread the news!

the shield of faith – be obedient in faith!

the helmet of salvation – take every thought captive.

the sword of the Spirit – learn to wield the Word of God.

Hymn or song _____

_____

_____

This is Your day, Lord, and I am Yours in it!

◯ face-time with Jesus

Pray:
& Praise
_____

_____

Repent:
& He will give peace
_____

_____

Ask:
pour out your heart
_____

_____

Yes:
stand on His promises
_____

_____

Doodles & Notes

He makes all things beautiful in His time.

Jesus, I trust you with...

_____

_____

_____

_____

Handwritten Scripture

what I learned

⭐ armor check

the belt of truth – stand firm on what God says!
the breastplate of righteousness – holiness given/holiness lived.
the shoes of peace – stand firm, spread the news!
the shield of faith – be obedient in faith!
the helmet of salvation – take every thought captive.
the sword of the Spirit – learn to wield the Word of God.

on the third day, He will come like rain.
Hosea 6:3

hymn or song:
_____
_____

◯ face-time with Jesus

P R A Y & P R A I S E
_____
_____

R E P E N T receive forgiveness
_____
_____

A S K He hears
_____
_____

Y E S Thank you, Jesus!
_____
_____

HE MAKES BEAUTY FROM ASHES ——>
JESUS, I TRUST YOU WITH:
_____
_____
_____
_____

Notes & Doodles

Handwritten Scripture

▶ *what I learned*

○ armor check

the belt of truth – stand firm on what God says!

the breastplate of righteousness – holiness given/holiness lived.

the shoes of peace – stand firm, spread the news!

the shield of faith – be obedient in faith!

the helmet of salvation – take every thought captive.

the sword of the Spirit – learn to wield the Word of God.

This hope is a strong and trustworthy anchor for our souls. It leads us through the curtain into God's inner sanctuary.
Hebrews 6:19

hymn or song:
_____
_____
_____

▲ ☐ face-time with Jesus

Pray:
& Praise
_____
_____

Repent:
He gives grace
_____
_____

Ask:
& He will answer
_____
_____

Yes:
He will never leave you
_____
_____

Our struggle is not against flesh and blood.
Jesus, I trust you with:
_____
_____
_____
_____

Notes & Doodles

Handwritten Scripture

what I learned...

☆ armor check

the belt of truth – stand firm on what God says!

the breastplate of righteousness – holiness given/holiness lived.

the shoes of peace – stand firm, spread the news!

the shield of faith – be obedient in faith!

the helmet of salvation – take every thought captive.

the sword of the Spirit – learn to wield the Word of God.

Grace received...Grace given.

hymn or song:

_____

_____

_____

○ **face-time with Jesus**

Pray: _____
& Praise _____

_____

Repent:_____
He will come like the rain

_____

Ask: _____
let your request be known

_____

Yes: _____
He's a good Father

_____

Mercy Triumphs
JESUS, I TRUST YOU WITH:

◄ **Notes & Doodles**

_____

_____

_____

_____

_____

Handwritten Scripture

_____

_____

_____

_____

_____

_____

_____

_____

_____

_____

_____

WHaT I LearNeD ToDay...

_____

_____

_____

_____

⬭ armor check

the belt of truth – stand firm on what God says!

the breastplate of righteousness – holiness given/holiness lived.

the shoes of peace – stand firm, spread the news!

the shield of faith – be obedient in faith!

the helmet of salvation – take every thought captive.

the sword of the Spirit – learn to wield the Word of God.

BLESSED iS SHE
WHOSE STRENGTH
iS THE LORD!

hymn or song:

_____

_____

face-time with Jesus

Pray: & Praise _____

_____

Repent: _____
His blood covers it all

_____

Ask: _____
and you will receive

_____

Yes: _____
His blessings are amazing

_____

Control is an illusion > God has it.
Jesus, I trust you with:

_____

_____

_____

_____

Notes & Doodles

Handwritten Scripture

_____

_____

_____

_____

_____

_____

_____

_____

_____

_____

_____

_____

_____ what I learned

_____

_____

_____

⃝armor check

the belt of truth – stand firm on what God says!

the breastplate of righteousness – holiness given/holiness lived.

the shoes of peace – stand firm, spread the news!

the shield of faith – be obedient in faith!

the helmet of salvation – take every thought captive.

the sword of the Spirit – learn to wield the Word of God.

Hymn or Song _____

_____

➤ face-time with Jesus

Blessed is she
whose strength
is in the Lord.

Pray: _____
& Praise

_____

Repent: _____
strength is in forgiveness

_____

Ask: _____
the Shepherd gives us what we need

_____

Yes: _____
take Him at His Word

_____

NOTES & DOODLES

Jesus, I trust you with...
Your grace is sufficient.

_____

_____

_____

_____

_____

Handwritten Scripture

_____
_____
_____
_____
_____
_____
_____
_____
_____
_____

what I learned ——→
_____
_____
_____
_____

☐ ARMOR CHECK
the belt of truth – stand firm on what God says!
the breastplate of righteousness – holiness given/holiness lived.
the shoes of peace – stand firm, spread the news!
the shield of faith – be obedient in faith!
the helmet of salvation – take every thought captive.
the sword of the Spirit – learn to wield the Word of God.

HYMN or song _____
_____
_____

face-time with Jesus ⬅

Dare to live in the
freedom Christ
died to give you.

Pray: _____
& Praise _____

Repent: _____
give it to Jesus _____

Ask: _____
He is listening _____

Yes: _____
His plan is good _____

_____

He loves me, this I know.

JESUS, I TrUST YOU WITH...

_____

_____

_____

_____

Doodles & Notes

Handwritten Scripture

what I learned

⭕ armor check

the belt of truth – stand firm on what God says!

the breastplate of righteousness – holiness given/holiness lived.

the shoes of peace – stand firm, spread the news!

the shield of faith – be obedient in faith!

the helmet of salvation – take every thought captive.

the sword of the Spirit – learn to wield the Word of God.

HYMN OR SONG _____

_____

_____

face-time with Jesus

Pray: _____
& Praise

_____

Repent: _____
Create in me a clean heart!

_____

Ask: _____
all I have needed, Your hand has provided

_____

Yes: _____
Your Word is light to my path

_____

notes & doodles

Sadness to joy
Tiredness to dancing.
Sin-sick to healed.
All because of Jesus.

Jesus, I trust you with...
He is our peace.

_____

_____

_____

_____

_____

Handwritten Scripture

_____
_____
_____
_____
_____
_____
_____
_____
_____
_____
_____
_____

what I learned

_____
_____
_____
_____

☐ armor check

the belt of truth – stand firm on what God says!
the breastplate of righteousness – holiness given/holiness lived.
the shoes of peace – stand firm, spread the news!
the shield of faith – be obedient in faith!
the helmet of salvation – take every thought captive.
the sword of the Spirit – learn to wield the Word of God.

Hymn or song _____

_____

_____

This is Your day, Lord, and I am Yours in it!

◯ face-time with Jesus

Pray:
& Praise
_____

_____

Repent:
& He will give peace
_____

_____

Ask:
pour out your heart
_____

_____

Yes:
stand on His promises
_____

_____

Doodles & Notes

He makes all things beautiful in His time.

Jesus, I trust you with...

_____

_____

_____

_____

Handwritten Scripture

what I learned

⭐ armor check

the belt of truth – stand firm on what God says!
the breastplate of righteousness – holiness given/holiness lived.
the shoes of peace – stand firm, spread the news!
the shield of faith – be obedient in faith!
the helmet of salvation – take every thought captive.
the sword of the Spirit – learn to wield the Word of God.

This hope is a strong and trustworthy anchor for our souls. It leads us through the curtain into God's inner sanctuary.

Hebrews 6:19

hymn or song:

_____

_____

_____

▲ ☐ face-time with Jesus

Pray:
& Praise

_____

Repent:
He gives grace

_____

Ask:
& He will answer

_____

Yes:
He will never leave you

_____

Our struggle is not against flesh and blood.

Jesus, I trust you with:

_____

Notes & Doodles

Handwritten Scripture

_____

_____

_____

_____

_____

_____

_____

_____

_____

_____

what I learned...

_____

_____

_____

⭐ armor check

the belt of truth - stand firm on what God says!

the breastplate of righteousness - holiness given/holiness lived.

the shoes of peace - stand firm, spread the news!

the shield of faith - be obedient in faith!

the helmet of salvation - take every thought captive.

the sword of the Spirit - learn to wield the Word of God.

Grace received...Grace given.

_____

_____

_____

◯ **face-time with Jesus**

Pray: _____
& Praise
_____

Repent: _____
He will come like the rain
_____

Ask: _____
let your request be known
_____

Yes: _____
He's a good Father
_____

Mercy Triumphs
JESUS, I TRUST YOU WITH:

◄ **Notes & Doodles**

_____

_____

_____

_____

_____

Handwritten Scripture

What I Learned Today...

◯ armor check

the belt of truth – stand firm on what God says!
the breastplate of righteousness – holiness given/holiness lived.
the shoes of peace – stand firm, spread the news!
the shield of faith – be obedient in faith!
the helmet of salvation – take every thought captive.
the sword of the Spirit – learn to wield the Word of God.

BLESSED IS SHE
WHOSE STRENGTH
IS THE LORD!

hymn or song:

_____

_____

face-time with Jesus

Pray: _____
& Praise

_____

Repent: _____
His blood covers it all

_____

Ask: _____
and you will receive

_____

Yes: _____
His blessings are amazing

_____

Control is an illusion > God has it.
Jesus, I trust you with:

_____

_____

_____

_____

Notes & Doodles

Handwritten Scripture

what I learned

armor check

the belt of truth - stand firm on what God says!

the breastplate of righteousness - holiness given/holiness lived.

the shoes of peace - stand firm, spread the news!

the shield of faith - be obedient in faith!

the helmet of salvation - take every thought captive.

the sword of the Spirit - learn to wield the Word of God.

Hymn or Song _____

_____

➡ face-time with Jesus

Pray: _____
& Praise

Repent: _____
strength is in forgiveness

Ask: _____
the Shepherd gives us what we need

Yes: _____
take Him at His Word

NOTES & DOODLES

Blessed is she
whose strength
is in the Lord.

Jesus, I trust you with...
Your grace is sufficient.

_____

_____

_____

_____

_____

Handwritten Scripture

_____
_____
_____
_____
_____
_____
_____
_____
_____
_____
_____

what I learned →

_____
_____
_____
_____

☐ ARMOR CHECK

the belt of truth – stand firm on what God says!
the breastplate of righteousness – holiness given/holiness lived.
the shoes of peace – stand firm, spread the news!
the shield of faith – be obedient in faith!
the helmet of salvation – take every thought captive.
the sword of the Spirit – learn to wield the Word of God.

Hymn or song _____

_____

face-time with Jesus ⬅

Dare to live in the freedom Christ died to give you.

Pray: _____
  & Praise

_____

Repent: _____
  give it to Jesus

_____

Ask: _____
  He is listening

_____

Yes: _____
  His plan is good

_____

He loves me, this I know.

Doodles & Notes

JESUS, I TRUST YOU WITH...

_____

_____

_____

_____

Handwritten Scripture

what I learned

◯ armor check

the belt of truth - stand firm on what God says!

the breastplate of righteousness - holiness given/holiness lived.

the shoes of peace - stand firm, spread the news!

the shield of faith - be obedient in faith!

the helmet of salvation - take every thought captive.

the sword of the Spirit - learn to wield the Word of God.

HYmn or song _____

_____

🌿 face-time with Jesus

Pray: _____
& Praise

_____

Repent: _____
Create in me a clean heart!

_____

Ask: _____
all I have needed, Your hand has provided

_____

Yes: _____
Your Word is light to my path

_____

notes & doodles

Sadness to joy
Tiredness to dancing.
Sin-sick to healed.
🌿 All because of Jesus 🌿

Jesus, I trust you with...
He is our peace.

_____

_____

_____

_____

_____

Handwritten Scripture

_____
_____
_____
_____
_____
_____
_____
_____
_____
_____
_____

what I learned

_____
_____
_____
_____

☐ armor check

the belt of truth – stand firm on what God says!

the breastplate of righteousness – holiness given/holiness lived.

the shoes of peace – stand firm, spread the news!

the shield of faith – be obedient in faith!

the helmet of salvation – take every thought captive.

the sword of the Spirit – learn to wield the Word of God.

other notes & thoughts:

Made in the USA
Charleston, SC
04 August 2016